GUESSWORKS!

GUESSWORKS!

A Musical Mystery Play

Text, Music, and Lyrics by
HOWARD BECKERMAN
Hunter College, City University of New York

Illustrations by
GATOT P. BOEDIMAN

A Theatrical
Listening-Based Textbook & Cassette
with Integrated Activities for
Intermediate ESL Classes

COLLIER
MACMILLAN

Collier Macmillan Canada, Inc.

Printing: 1 2 3 4 5 6 7 Year: 9 0 1 2 3 4 5

Collier Macmillan
ESL/EFL Department
866 Third Avenue
New York, NY 10022
Printed in the U.S.A.
ISBN 0-02-307591-0

INTRODUCTION

Guessworks! is an unusual intermediate-level, **listening-based** text with integrated classroom activities. The material revolves around a **continuing suspense story,** presented in the form of a **musical play** — with the performance provided on an accompanying **audiocassette** and illustrated in the text.

Why a musical play for ESL? Besides the obvious benefits of using stimulating listening material as input for classroom activities, the fact that American musical theater has offered a unique contribution to world culture suggests this medium as one that deserves exploration in ESL programs. The author/composer of *Guessworks!* is a veteran ESL teacher and author — as well as a member of the Dramatists Guild.

Guessworks! presents a three-character musical play in eight scenes. The material assumes an initial exposure to basic structures and offers intermediate-level students an opportunity to develop their skills in an exciting context. The story involves confused identity, romance, and international intrigue.

Tasks invite students to participate actively in the unfolding drama (and comedy) by "guessing" about the characters and plot as they listen.

Guessworks! also lends itself well to informal (or formal) **classroom performance** by the students. Individual scenes may be rehearsed, or the entire play may be presented as a class project. Since there are only three characters, the teacher may wish to have several casts working simultaneously. The eight scenes of the play may be performed successfully without the songs, but for those teachers and students who are musically inclined, the **sheet music** for the eight songs is provided at the end of the text.

Guessworks! has been field-tested with adult and young adult ESL students at low-, mid-, and high-intermediate levels. The vocabulary of the scenes has been controlled so that the material is accessible to low-intermediate students; the songs are more idiomatically (though not lexically) sophisticated, and they provide a challenge for students at both the lower and higher ends of the intermediate spectrum.

The design of the activities, the intrigue of the story line, and the thrill of the musical theater genre make *Guessworks!* an exciting ESL experience.

Each of the eight *Guessworks!* units follows the plan outlined below. A dialogue scene serves as the core for activities **A** through **F**; a song is the core for activities **G** through **K**. And each of the two sections begins with an illustration to inspire guesswork about the scene or song to follow. Thus, the eight *Guessworks!* units are easily adaptable to provide *sixteen class lessons.*

 **A** **Previews**   Students look at a provocative illustration which previews the upcoming scene. In a free **discussion** and **writing** activity, they **guess**

about what they think will happen and share their interpretations with a partner.

B *Cues*

Students **listen** to selected sentences (read by the teacher) from the scene they are about to hear. (The teacher can find the sentences to read in the Answer Key.) In a choice exercise, students circle the sentence that they hear. The sentences in this exercise are chosen to help students at this level learn to hear reductions of unstressed vowels and selected phonemic contrasts.

C *Scene*

Students **listen** to the scene and complete one or more listening tasks. These include listening for main ideas, specific details, tone, sequence, vocabulary meanings in context, and pronoun references. Tasks also focus on listening in order to make inferences, draw conclusions, and recognize attitudes. Students then listen to the scene as they follow the script in the text. Then, in small groups or pairs, they compare their answers to the listening exercises.

D *Improvisation*

In a **role-playing** activity, students enact their own scenes based on the context of the play.

E *Themes*

In a **discussion** activity, students talk about their own feelings and ideas on themes that are related to the context of the scene.

F *Spotlight 1*

In a vocabulary, grammar, or pronunciation activity, students focus on **language** in the script.

G *Overture*

Students look at an illustration which previews the ideas and/or emotions in the "show tune" that they are about to hear. They **guess** what they think the character will sing about and **discuss** their reactions.

H *Song*

Students **listen** to the song, which arises naturally from the context of the scene. As they listen, they follow the lyrics in the text and fill in missing words (verb forms, prepositions, articles, pronouns, etc.).

I *Reviews*

Questions for class **discussion** follow the song.

J *Spotlight 2*

In a vocabulary, grammar, or pronunciation activity, students focus on **language** in the song.

K *Finale*

A final **writing** activity provides another opportunity for "guesswork."

CONTENTS

Scene 1

Strangers 2

Scene 2

Just Around the Corner 14

H.	*Song*	Listening for Articles and Prepositions
I.	*Reviews*	Discussion
J.	*Spotlight 2*	Idioms and Vocabulary in Context
K.	*Finale*	Guesswork

Scene 3

Mr. Nice Guy 24

Scene 4

Late Last Night 36

Scene 5

Mind Game 46

Scene 6

I Am Not the Man 56

Scene 7

Scene 8

ACKNOWLEDGMENTS

I wish to express my thanks to the many persons who have helped to bring this project to publication.

At the International English Language Institute of Hunter College, City University of New York: Pamela McPartland, for many years of enthusiastic encouragement and counsel; Peter Thomas, whose talents in both the theatrical and English-teaching arts have been an inspiration; and my many colleagues at the Institute, for their friendship and support.

At the Collier Macmillan ESL/EFL Department: Mary Jane Peluso, whose sense of vision helped make a dream come true; Maggie Scarry, who refused to let me forget a deadline or a detail; Agatha Lorenzo, for her help with the organization of units; Kathy Niemczyk, for her eye on consistency; and Karen Peratt, Director of the ESL/EFL Department, for her confidence and kindness.

At Heartworks: Linda Zoblotsky and Lou Davidson for their wonderful performances as Vi and Frank on the cassette; my children, Shira, Joshua, and Briana, for their support; and especially my wife, Linda, my partner in time and love, and my best friend.

H.B.

GUESSWORKS!

STRANGERS

A Previews

1. With a partner, **talk** about what you see in the picture on the next page. **Guess** what's happening.
2. By yourself, **write** a paragraph about the picture.

_____
_____
_____
_____
_____
_____
_____
_____
_____
_____

3. When you finish, **exchange** paragraphs with your partner. **Read** your partner's paragraph and **check** for errors. If you don't understand something, **ask** your partner about it. If you find a mistake, help your partner to **fix** it.

B Cues

Your teacher will read some sentences. You will hear these words in the next scene. **Listen carefully** *and circle the letter of the sentence that you hear. Your teacher will say each one twice. The first one is done for you.*

1. a. Where were you going?
    b. Were you going?
    ©   Where are you going?

2. a. I'm not at the shore.
    b. And not yours.
    c. I'm not sure.

3. a. How are you?
    b. Who are you?
    c. How were you?

4. a. Where do you live?
    b. Where did you live?
    c. When do you leave?

5. a. Were you home?
    b. Where's your home?
    c. Where is her home?

6. a. Try to think.
    b. Try this thing.
    c. Try the thing.

7. a. No, it's long.
    b. I know it's long.
    c. I know I'm alone.

8. a. You are not alone.
    b. You were not long.
    c. You're not in London.

9. a. I'm hearing you.
    b. I'm here with you.
    c. And how are you?

10. a. Can he stay with me?
    b. Can you stay with me?
    c. Kenny's day with me.

Your teacher will tell you the answers and may ask you to **repeat** *sentences that were difficult for you to hear correctly.*

C Scene

Listening for Main Ideas

*First read these two questions. Then listen to the scene once and circle **a**, **b**, **c**, or **d**.*

1. What does the woman want?

   a. To call the police.   c. To help the man.
   b. To find the right train.   d. To remember the man's name.

2. What does the man want?

   a. To stay with the woman.   c. To be alone.
   b. To get on a train.   d. To find his family.

Listening for Details

Listen to the scene a second time to complete the rest of the exercise.

3. The woman asks a lot of questions. Check (√) the ones that you hear.

   _____   a.   Are you feeling O.K.?
   _____   b.   Can I do something for you?
   _____   c.   Which train do you want?
   _____   d.   Where are you going?
   _____   e.   How are you?
   _____   f.   Who are you?
   _____   g.   What's your name?
   _____   h.   Are you happy?
   _____   i.   Are you alone?
   _____   j.   Do you have a family?

4. The man asks only one question. Write it here.

   _____

Now listen for the last time while you follow the script below.

Scene 1

[A train passes.]

1	Woman:	Excuse me. Are you feeling O.K.?
2	Man:	I don't know.
3	Woman:	Can I do something for you?
4	Man:	I don't know. I feel very strange.
5	Woman:	Are you waiting for the next train?
6	Man:	I'm not sure.
7	Woman:	Well, where are you going?
8	Man:	Nowhere.
9	Woman:	Who are you?
10	Man:	What?
11	Woman:	What's your name?
12	Man:	My name? My name . . . I don't know my name!
13	Woman:	Where do you live?
14	Man:	Live?
15	Woman:	Where's your home?
16	Man:	Home . . . I don't remember.
17	Woman:	Now try to think. Do you have a family?
18		Maybe a wife . . . or a girlfriend?
19	Man:	No. I think . . . No, I know I'm alone.
20	Woman:	You are not alone. I'm here with you.

[A train arrives.]

21	Man:	Can you stay with me?

Now double-check your answers in Part C and compare your answers with a partner's.

D Improvisation

1. With a partner, make two lists of adjectives—one to describe the man's feelings and the other to describe the woman's. Then your teacher will write some of your adjectives on the board.

The Man	The Woman
_____	_____

2. Now choose one student to be the man and another to be the woman. They can read Scene 1 aloud and then put the book down and **continue** the conversation between the man and the woman at the train station. To help with the acting, the students may choose one or two of the adjectives from the class's lists and use them to help create their characters.

3. The rest of the class can be other people in the subway. Join the man and the woman and try to find out more about their story. Ask lots of questions!

E Themes

In small groups or as a whole class, discuss your answers to these questions:

1. Do you often start conversations with strangers? Why or why not?
2. Do you make friends easily? Why or why not?
3. Make some suggestions about how to make new friends in the city or town where you are now.
4. Describe your best friend.

F Spotlight 1

Scanning for Synonyms

Work with a partner. Look in the script for Scene 1 to find words with these meanings and write them in the spaces. Also, write the number of the line where you find the word.

1. by myself _____ (line ____)
2. not anyplace _____ (line ____)
3. perhaps _____ (line ____)
4. unusual _____ (line ____)

5. pardon _____ (line ____)
6. certain _____ (line ____)
7. may _____ (line ____)
8. all right _____ (line ____)

G Overture

Before you listen to the song, look at the picture below. Try to **guess** what the man and the woman will sing about. How are they feeling? What are they thinking? Why do you think so? Discuss your ideas as a whole class.

H Song

*Now listen to the song and fill in the missing **verb forms**. You may listen as many times as you like.*

Strangers

Woman:
1 Strangers,
2 Are we really strangers?
3 So suddenly I _____ a friend,
4 Or am I _____ only what I want to _____?
5 Sometimes I let a dream take all of me.

6 Strangers,
7 _____ hands with strangers
8 Is something new and magical.
9 I wonder if he _____ how much I _____ to _____.
10 Sometimes I let a dream take all my day.

11 And maybe tomorrow we'll _____ together.
12 Maybe tomorrow he'll _____ his dream.
13 And maybe tomorrow
14 I'll _____ whether this stranger is my friend.
15 I'll _____ his story from the start.
16 I'll _____ a very special part
17 In the end.

Man:
18 Strangers,
19 _____ to be with strangers.
20 There's nothing more appealing than
21 A kindness _____ through you from a stranger's smile.
22 Sometimes I let a dream take hold awhile.

Woman:
23 Strangers,
24 Good to be with strangers.
25 _____ this myst'ry man,
26 Uncovering the woman I am soon to be,
27 Sometimes I let a dream take care of me.

Together:
28 So maybe tomorrow we'll _____ together.

Woman:
29 Maybe tomorrow he'll _____ his dream.

Man:
30 And maybe tomorrow
31 I'll _____ whether this stranger is my friend.

Woman:
32 I'll _____ his story from the start.

Man:
33 I'll _____ a very special part

Together:
34 In the end.

Woman:
35 Strangers,
36 Are we really _____ hands?

Man:
37 Strangers,
38 _____ to be with, good to be

Together:
39 Strangers.

I Reviews

Discuss your answers to these questions with the whole class.

1. Are the woman and the man singing to each other or to themselves? How do you know?
2. What do we learn about them from this song? How do they feel about each other? About themselves?
3. In line 19, what do you think "born to be with strangers" means?

J Spotlight 2

Indirect Yes/No Questions

In line 9 of the song, the woman sings, "I wonder if he knows how much I need to stay." She is asking herself, "Does he know how much I need to stay?"

PART ONE

Work with a partner. Write more yes/no questions that the man and woman might have about each other.

The Man

1. *Does she live near the station?*
2. _____
3. _____
4. _____
5. _____

The Woman

1. *Is he married?*
2. _____
3. _____
4. _____
5. _____

PART TWO

Now fill in the blanks to rewrite the questions that you just wrote in the boxes.

The Man

1. The man **wonders** *if she lives near the station* _____.
2. He **doesn't know** _____.
3. He **isn't sure** _____.
4. He **wants to know** _____.
5. He **asks himself** _____.

The Woman

1. The woman **wonders** *if he is married* _____.
2. She **would like to know** _____.
3. She **isn't sure** _____.
4. She **wants to know** _____.
5. She **asks herself** _____.

PART THREE

For conversation with a partner: **I wonder if** _____.

> What do *you* wonder about *other students in your class?* Talk about things you would really like to know. If your partner can't give you the information, *guess!*

K *Finale*

What do you think will happen in the next scene? Describe three very different possibilities—one sentence for each.

Possibility #1: *Maybe the man and the woman will* _____
_____.

Possibility #2: _____
_____.

Possibility #3: _____
_____.

In small groups or as a whole class, share your guesses with your classmates.

JUST AROUND THE CORNER

A Previews

1. With a partner, **talk** about what you see in the picture on the next page. **Guess** what's happening.
2. By yourself, **write** a paragraph about the picture.

_____
_____
_____
_____
_____
_____
_____
_____
_____
_____

3. When you finish, **exchange** paragraphs with your partner. **Read** your partner's paragraph and **check** for errors. If you don't understand something, **ask** your partner about it. If you find a mistake, help your partner to **fix** it.

B Cues

*Your teacher will read some sentences. You will hear these words in the next scene. **Listen carefully** and circle the letter of the sentence that you hear. Your teacher will say each one twice.*

1. a. Do you like to take a walk?
   b. Did you like to take a walk?
   c. Would you like to take a walk?

2. a. I can continue.
   b. I can't continue.
   c. I can't. Can you?

3. a. You can decide.
   b. I could decide.
   c. Look on the side.

4. a. You have some help for me.
   b. You have to help me.
   c. You haven't helped me.

5. a. What's a favorite color?
   b. What's her favorite color?
   c. What's your favorite color?

6. a. You remember something.
   b. You remembered something.
   c. You'll remember something.

7. a. I like it.
   b. I liked it.
   c. I like that.

8. a. Next, I'll meet you.
   b. Nice to meet her.
   c. Nice to meet you.

9. a. You did it again.
   b. You didn't care.
   c. You did and you can.

10. a. I want to talk to you.
    b. I wanted to talk to you.
    c. I want it told to you.

*Your teacher will tell you the answers and may ask you to **repeat** sentences that were difficult for you to hear correctly.*

C Scene

Listening for Feelings and Main Ideas

*First read these two questions. Then listen to the scene once and circle **a**, **b**, **c**, or **d**.*

1. At the end of this scene, which is *not* true?

   a. Whitey likes Vi.
   b. Vi likes Whitey.
   c. Whitey feels that something good will happen.
   d. Vi feels sorry that Whitey doesn't want to eat.

2. Which is true?

   a. The man's real name is Whitey, and the woman's real name is Violet.
   b. The man's real name isn't Whitey, and the woman's real name isn't Violet.
   c. The man's real name is Whitey, but the woman's real name isn't Violet.
   d. The man's real name isn't Whitey, but the woman's real name is Violet.

Listening for Details

What does the man remember in this scene? Listen again and then check (√) all of the things that he remembers.

3. _____ a. his real name   _____ d. his address
   _____ b. his favorite color   _____ e. his favorite restaurant
   _____ c. his favorite food   _____ f. his favorite corner

Listening for References

*Listen to the scene a third time. When you hear the six sentences below, choose the correct meaning of the words in **bold print** and circle **a** or **b**. If necessary, you may listen a fourth time for these answers.*

4. **That**'s all the colors together.

   a. a rainbow   b. white light

5. I like **it**.

   a. the name Whitey   b. the color white

6. I think **so**.

   a. not very much   b. I'm hungry

7. You **did it** again.

   a. remembered something   b. ate something

8. And maybe **that**'ll help you remember the rest of your life.

   a. remembering something   b. getting some soup

9. Well, I'm glad you **did**.

   a. knew the truth   b. talked to me

Now listen for the last time while you follow the script below.

Scene 2

1	Woman:	Would you like to take a walk with me?
2	Man:	Why not?

[They walk up the stairs.]

3	Woman:	Well, I can't continue to talk to you without
4		a name. What name would you like?
5	Man:	You can decide.
6	Woman:	All right. But you have to help me. What's your
7		favorite color?
8	Man:	White. I thought of white light. That's all the
9		colors together.
10	Woman:	Wonderful! You remembered something! You
11		didn't have to stop and think about it. White . . .
12		We'll call you "Whitey."
13	Whitey:	I like it. But why did you want to use a color?
14	Woman:	My name's Violet. Just call me Vi.
15	Whitey:	Hi, Vi. Nice to meet you.
16	Vi:	Nice to meet you, too. Now . . . Are you hungry?
17	Whitey:	I think so.
18	Vi:	What's your favorite food?
19	Whitey:	Wonton soup.
20	Vi:	You did it again! You remembered something
21		else! Come on, Whitey. There's a Chinese
22		restaurant around the corner. We'll get you some
23		soup. And maybe that'll help you remember the
24		rest of your life.
25	Whitey:	I'm a lucky guy, Vi. You're very kind.
26	Vi:	Not really. The truth is—as soon as I saw you,
27		I knew that I wanted to talk to you.
28	Whitey:	Well, I'm glad you did. And I have a feeling
29		that today . . . something wonderful is going
30		to happen!

Now double-check your answers in Part C and compare your answers with a partner's.

D Improvisation

Work in pairs to complete the following role-playing plan. Practice your scene, and then you can act it out.

You are two strangers who meet _____. You begin to talk about _____, and
　　　　　　　　　　　　　　　　　　(where?)　　　　　　　　　　　　　　　　　　　(what?)
then you both decide _____.
　　　　　　　　　　　(to do what?)

E Themes

In small groups or as a whole class, discuss your answers to these questions:

1. Do you have a nickname? What is it? How did you get it? Do you like it?
2. If you could change your name to anything at all, what name would you like? Why?
3. What are your favorites? Favorite color? Favorite food? Favorite place?

F Spotlight 1

Pronunciation: *can / can't*

*Listen to the beginning of Scene 2 once more. Listen for the pronunciation of **can't** (in line 3) and **can** (in line 5). Compare the pronunciation of the letter **a** in **can't** and **can**. Do you hear the difference?*

The *a* in c**a**n (the positive auxiliary) is reduced—it is not pronounced completely. But the *a* in c**a**n't (the negative auxiliary) is completely clear. Also, the negative form is stressed (stronger), but the positive form is unstressed (weaker).

---

1. With a partner, practice pronouncing the pairs of sentences below.
   Example: You can decide / You can't decide. (You c**a**n de**cide**. / You **can't** decide.)

   a. I can go. / I can't go.　　　　　　c. I can help you. / I can't help you.
   b. We can do it. / We can't do it.　　d. You can take it. / You can't take it.

2. Say (but don't write) these sentences for your partner and complete them with *true facts about yourself*. Then your partner will ask you some questions to get more information about what you said.

   a. I bet you didn't know that I can _____.
   b. I bet you didn't know that I can't _____.
   c. I'm happy that I can remember _____.
   d. I'm happy that I can't remember _____.

G Overture

*Before you listen to the song, look at the picture below. Try to **guess** what Vi will sing about. How are they both feeling? What are they thinking? Why do you think so? Discuss your ideas as a whole class.*

H Song

Now listen to the song and fill in the missing **articles** and **prepositions**. You may listen as many times as you like.

Just Around the Corner

Vi:
1   Just around the corner, _____ surprise or two.
2   Just around the corner, there's _____ answer for you.
3   Step alive, step alive,
4   Any moment you arrive, _____ coast is clear.
5   _____ truth is just
6   Around the corner, 'round the corner
7   Right here!

8   Just around the corner, _____ idea or two.
9   Just around the corner, there's _____ mem'ry _____ you.
10   Look alive, look alive,
11   And _____ image will arrive to fill your mind.
12   Don't leave _____ picture
13   ('Round the corner, 'round the corner)
14   Behind.

15   Arm _____ arm,
16   Heart _____ heart,
17   You can tell _____ worlds apart.
18   Eye _____ eye,
19   Soul _____ soul,
20   Take it easy
21   As you stroll.

22	Just around the corner, play _____ game or two.
23	Just around the corner, there's _____ grand prize for you.
24	Come alive, come alive,
25	As _____ winner you'll arrive to take your place.
26	So if you're movin'
27	'Round the corner, 'round the corner,
28	Keep pace!
29	Left, right, left, right!
30	What is left?
31	Well, you're all right.
32	Just around the corner!
33	You're invited _____ _____ party tonight!
34	Just around the corner!

ⓘ Reviews

Discuss your answers to these questions with the whole class.

1. What is Vi's main idea in this song? Say it in your own words—in one sentence.
2. Did you ever win a prize? For what?
3. When we say something is "just around the corner" we sometimes mean that it will happen very soon. What changes are "just around the corner" in *your* life?

Ⓙ Spotlight 2

Idioms and Vocabulary in Context

PART ONE

Try to match the vocabulary and idioms in the song with their meanings at the right. Write the correct letter in the space to the left of the number.

_____	1. step alive (line 3)	a. relax
_____	2. the coast is clear (line 4)	b. stay at the same speed as others
_____	3. look alive (line 10)	c. take a slow walk

_____ 4. tell _____ apart (line 17)   d. walk quickly

_____ 5. soul (line 19)   e. nobody is in sight

_____ 6. take it easy (line 20)   f. see the difference

_____ 7. stroll (line 21)   g. pay attention

_____ 8. come alive (line 24)   h. personal spirit

_____ 9. keep pace (line 28)   i. begin to feel a lot of energy

PART TWO

Decide whether or not each of the following statements is logical. Write **L** (logical) or **I** (illogical) in the space to the left of the number.

_____ 1. I was late, so I decided to **stroll** to work.

_____ 2. I worked hard all day, so I need to **take it easy** tonight.

_____ 3. Many people believe that the **soul** never dies.

_____ 4. The twin brothers do not look alike, so nobody can **tell** them **apart**.

_____ 5. **Step alive!** You're moving too slowly!

_____ 6. **Look alive!** Try not to fall asleep when the teacher is talking.

_____ 7. The audience will **come alive** as soon as the star walks onto the stage.

_____ 8. Children, try to **keep pace** with the rest of us. We don't want anyone to get lost.

_____ 9. "**The coast is clear**," said one robber to the other. "We can't run away yet."

K _Finale_

At the end of Scene 2, Whitey feels that "something wonderful is going to happen." And Vi sings that there will be a surprise "just around the corner." What do you think will happen in the next scene? Write your **guesses** below.

_____

_____

_____

_____

_____

_____

_____

_____

_____

_____

In small groups or as a whole class, share your guesses with your classmates.

MR. NICE GUY

A Previews

1. With a partner, **talk** about what you see in the picture on the next page. **Guess** what's happening.
2. By yourself, **write** a paragraph about the picture.

_____
_____
_____
_____
_____
_____
_____
_____
_____
_____

3. When you finish, **exchange** paragraphs with your partner. **Read** your partner's paragraph and **check** for errors. If you don't understand something, **ask** your partner about it. If you find a mistake, help your partner to **fix** it.

B Cues

Your teacher will read some sentences or phrases. You will hear these words in the next scene. **Listen carefully** *and circle the letter of the sentence or phrase that you hear. Your teacher will say each one twice.*

1. a. Are you still angry?
   b. Are you still hungry?
   c. Are you still ugly?

2. a. We have to find it.
   b. We have to find art.
   c. We have to find out.

3. a. We should go.
   b. We shouldn't go.
   c. Wish you'd go.

4. a. I remember everything.
   b. I'll remember everything.
   c. I remembered everything.

5. a. I don't want to use you.
   b. I don't want to lose you.
   c. I don't want a new zoo.

6. a. I'll never see you again.
   b. I never see if you can.
   c. I'll never see your gun.

7. a. That's not a shoe.
   b. That's not you.
   c. That's not true.

8. a. I want to be your friend.
   b. I want a beer, friend.
   c. I won't be a friend.

9. a. We'll call all the police.
   b. We'll go to the police.
   c. Record it all, please.

10. a. Can I stay?
    b. Can't I stay?
    c. A nice day.

Your teacher will tell you the answers and may ask you to **repeat** *sentences that were difficult for you to hear correctly.*

C Scene

Listening for Attitude

First read these two questions. Then listen to the scene once and circle ***a***, ***b***, ***c***, *or* ***d***.

1. How does Whitey feel about answering Vi's questions?

   a. He is glad to.
   b. He doesn't want to.
   c. He wants to, but he can't.

2. How do they both feel about going to the police?

    a. Both of them want to go.
    b. Both of them don't want to go.
    c. Whitey wants to go, but Vi doesn't.
    d. Vi wants to go, but Whitey doesn't.

Listening for Sequence

*What is the **order** of Whitey and Vi's conversation in this scene? Listen one or two more times, and then write the letters **a**, **b**, **c**, **d**, and **e** in the space before each sentence (**a** happens first, **b** second, etc.).*

3. _____ Whitey says he will go to the police.
   _____ Vi asks about Whitey's house.
   _____ Whitey shouts at Vi.
   _____ Whitey asks Vi one question.
   _____ Vi suggests going to the police.

Listening to Make Inferences

*Listen to the scene again and then circle **a**, **b**, **c**, or **d**.*

4. This scene happens _____.

    a. in the afternoon   c. in the morning
    b. at night   d. twenty-four hours after Whitey and Vi met each other

5. Vi believes that the police can _____.

    a. arrest Whitey
    b. find Whitey's family
    c. give Whitey some money

6. Whitey asks Vi one question. Write his question here.

   _____

   What is Vi's immediate reaction to this question?

   a. She is surprised.
   b. She is happy.
   c. She is furious.

Now listen for the last time while you follow the script below.

Scene 3

1	Vi:	Are you still hungry?
2	Whitey:	No. That was a great meal. Thanks.
3	Vi:	So . . . Do you have any new memories? What
4		kind of house do you live in? Is it an apartment
5		building?
6	Whitey:	Vi, please don't ask me any more questions. Let's
7		just have a good time together . . . now.
8	Vi:	But we have to find out who you really are. I
9		think we should go to the police. Your family
10		probably called them about you.
11	Whitey:	NO! ABSOLUTELY NOT! I—I—I'll remember
12		everything . . . soon. I know I will. If you just
13		stay with me.
14	Vi:	Whitey, I'm staying right here. But I think we'll
15		save a lot of time with the help of the police.
16		Why don't you want to find out if they have any
17		information about you?
18	Whitey:	I—I—I don't want to lose you. If the police send
19		me home, I'll never see you again.
20	Vi:	That's not true, Whitey. I told you I want to be
21		your friend. Don't worry.
22	Whitey:	All right. Just give me twenty-four hours. If I
23		don't remember who I am by tomorrow night,
24		we'll go to the police. Can I stay at your house
25		tonight?
26	Vi:	WHAT?

Now double-check your answers in Part C and compare your answers with a partner's.

D Improvisation

Work with a group to prepare the following role-playing activity. Practice your scene, and then you can act it out for the class.

Whitey says he will go to the police tomorrow—if he doesn't remember who he is. Imagine that they are at the police station. One student is Whitey *or* Vi. The others are police officers. Whitey or Vi will explain the situation to the police, and the officers will tell them what to do.

E Themes

In small groups or as a whole class, discuss your answers to these questions:

1. Do you think Whitey is telling the truth? Why or why not?
2. Do you have a secret? Say something about yourself that no one in the class knows.

F Spotlight 1

Future Possibilities: Conditional Sentences with *if*

Look at the words in **bold print** in these two sentences from Scene 3:

- If the police **send** me home, **I'll** never **see** you again. (lines 18 and 19)
- If I **don't remember** who I am by tomorrow night, **we'll go** to the police. (lines 22–24)

To refer to future possibilities, use the **present form** of the verb that comes immediately after *if*; the other verb is in the future form.

The sentences are also correct in this order:

- **I'll** never **see** you again if the police **send** me home.
- **We'll go** to the police if I **don't remember** who I am by tomorrow night.

PART ONE

Read these sentences about Whitey and Vi and <u>underline</u> the correct form in the parentheses.

1. If Whitey (doesn't remember / won't remember) everything during the next twenty-four hours, they'll go to the police.
2. If Whitey (shouts / will shout) again, Vi (isn't / won't be) happy about it.
3. Maybe they (find out / 'll find out) Whitey's real name if they (go / will go) to the police.
4. If Vi (asks / will ask) more questions before tomorrow night, Whitey probably (doesn't want / won't want) to answer them.
5. We (are all / 'll all be) surprised if we (discover / will discover) that Whitey's real name is Whitey.
6. Whitey is worried that if he (leaves / will leave), he (never sees / 'll never see) Vi again.
7. Whitey (is glad / will be glad) if they (go / will go) to Vi's house.
8. Perhaps, if they (are / will be) at Vi's house, Whitey (remembers / will remember) more about his life.

PART TWO

*Say the following sentences to your partner, completing them with **true facts about yourself**. Refer to **future** time after the word **if**.*

1. I'll never tell _____ that I _____
   because **if** _____.
2. I'll never ask _____ this question: _____?
   I'd like to ask, but I can't because **if** _____
   _____.

G Overture

*Before you listen to the song, look at the picture below. Try to **guess** what Whitey and Vi will sing about. How are they feeling? Why do you think so? Discuss your ideas as a whole class.*

H Song

Now listen to the song and fill in the missing **pronouns** and **contractions**. You may listen as many times as you like.

Mr. Nice Guy

Whitey:

1 Look into _____ eyes.
2 Don't _____ see that _____ sincere
3 And incredibly bright?
4 Baby, tell me _____ might
5 Take _____ in for the night!

6 _____ Mr. Nice Guy.
7 _____ fun to have around.
8 _____ Mr. Nice Guy.
9 With _____, _____ safe and sound.
10 And if _____ need some pleasant conversation,
11 Talk to _____!
12 If _____ want a little inspiration,
13 _____ agree
14 There is only one companion,
15 And _____ _____ for free!
16 Don't pass _____ by!
17 Let _____ be _____ Mr. Nice Guy!

Vi:

18 This is all so new!
19 Sure, I trust _____,
20 But _____ cannot invite _____ to stay.
21 No! _____ some better way.
22 _____ just met _____ today!

Whitey:

23   _____ Mr. Nice Guy.

Vi:

24   _____ fun to have around.

Whitey:

25   _____ Mr.

Together:

26   Nice Guy.

Vi:

27   With _____, _____ safe and sound.

Whitey:

28   And if _____ need some pleasant conversation,
29   Talk to _____!

Vi:

30   If _____ want a little inspiration, _____ can see
31   There is only one companion, and _____ mine for free!

Whitey:

32   Don't pass _____ by!

Vi:

33   Let _____ be _____ Mr.

Whitey:

34   Let _____ be _____ Mr.

Together:

35   Nice Guy!

I Reviews

Discuss your answers to these questions with the whole class.

1. Whitey wants Vi to invite him to her house. In this song, he tries to convince her by telling her all the good things about himself. What are *your* most positive qualities—the best things about you? List as many good points as you can!
2. How does Vi feel at the *beginning* of the song and at the *end*? Does she make a decision? How do you know?

J *Spotlight 2*

Scanning for Vocabulary and Idioms

Work with a partner. Look in the song lyrics to find words or phrases with these meanings. Also, write the number of the line where you find the word.

1. someone who stays with you _____ (line ____)
2. enjoyable _____ (line ____)
3. nice _____ (line ____)
4. honest _____ (line ____)
5. unbelievably _____ (line ____)
6. a feeling that makes you do something _____ (line ____)
7. feeling protected and comfortable _____ (line ____)
8. near _____ (line ____)
9. believe _____ (line ____)

K Finale

Work with a partner. Write a scene to immediately follow the song.

Whitey:

      Vi:

Whitey:

      Vi:

Whitey:

      Vi:

Whitey:

      Vi:

Whitey:

      Vi:

Whitey:

      Vi:

Whitey:

      Vi:

When you finish, share your scene with your other classmates.

LATE LAST NIGHT

A Previews

1. With a partner, **talk** about what you see in the picture on the next page. **Guess** what's happening.
2. By yourself, **write** a paragraph about the picture.

_____
_____
_____
_____
_____
_____
_____
_____
_____
_____

3. When you finish, **exchange** paragraphs with your partner. **Read** your partner's paragraph and **check** for errors. If you don't understand something, **ask** your partner about it. If you find a mistake, help your partner to **fix** it.

B Cues

Your teacher will read some sentences or phrases. You will hear these words in the next scene. **Listen carefully** *and circle the letter of the sentence or phrase that you hear. Your teacher will say each one twice.*

1. a. Why don't you sit down?
   b. What did you send down?
   c. Won't you sit down?

2. a. I never drink.
   b. I'll never drink.
   c. I never drink it.

3. a. You remember you're a mother.
   b. You remember your mother.
   c. You remembered a mother.

4. a. I'll remember anyone's boys.
   b. I remember a woman's voice.
   c. I remember a woman's boss.

5. a. I can't see her face.
   b. I can see her face.
   c. I can see your face.

6. a. Get out of here.
   b. Get at the hair.
   c. Got all of her.

7. a. On it a while.
   b. I'd own a white.
   c. I don't know why.

8. a. You've gotten happy.
   b. You've got to help me.
   c. You got half of me.

9. a. Don't ask me to leave.
   b. Then ask me to leave.
   c. Don't ask me to live.

10. a. Then tell me the truth.
    b. Then tell me to choose.
    c. Don't tell me the truth.

Your teacher will tell you the answers and may ask you to **repeat** *sentences that were difficult for you to hear correctly.*

C Scene

Listening for Feelings in Sequence

Listen two times in order to find out the **order** *of Vi's feelings in this scene. Then write the letters* **a, b, c, d,** *and* **e** *in the space before each feeling or combination of feelings (* **a** *is first,* **b** *is second, etc.).*

1. _____ nervous and surprised   _____ calm and serious   _____ afraid
   _____ cheerful and friendly   _____ angry

Listening for Details in Sequence

Listen to the scene again, and then complete these sentences about Whitey.

2. Whitey says that when he was young, his _____ told him that _____ was bad for him. Then he says that he doesn't really remember her. He remembers a woman's _____, but he doesn't remember her _____.

Listening to Make Inferences and Draw Conclusions

Check (√) all of the sentences that are probably true, according to the information in this scene. You may listen again if you need to.

3. _____ a. Whitey really remembers his mother.
   _____ b. Whitey is going to tell Vi a story.
   _____ c. Whitey really wants to go to the police.
   _____ d. Whitey is going to leave Vi's apartment now.
   _____ e. Vi wants to hear more information from Whitey.
   _____ f. When Whitey first arrived at Vi's apartment, he expected to tell her more about his life.
   _____ g. Whitey really doesn't drink coffee.

Listening for Examples of Language Functions

Whitey and Vi make different kinds of suggestions in this scene, including offers, requests, and commands. Listen again for the words that they use to introduce each suggestion. You may listen as many times as you need to.

4. _____ sit down on the sofa?
5. _____ get some coffee?
6. _____ go to the police.
7. _____ help me.
8. _____ don't ask me to leave.

Now listen for the last time while you follow the script below.

Scene 4

1	Vi:	Well, this is my apartment.
2	Whitey:	It's beautiful. You're beautiful.
3	Vi:	Why don't you sit down on the sofa?
4		Should I get some coffee?
5	Whitey:	No, I never drink it. When I was young, my
6		mother always said coffee would stop me from
7		growing.
8	Vi:	Oh!
9	Whitey:	What?
10	Vi:	You remember your mother.
11	Whitey:	Oh. Well—no. I remember a woman's voice
12		saying that to me. But I can't see her face.
13	Vi:	Whitey, I don't know if I believe you. Something
14		about this feels all wrong . . . I don't think you
15		should be here. Let's go to the police—right now.
16	Whitey:	STOP TALKING ABOUT THE POLICE!!
17	Vi:	Get out. I'm afraid of you. Get out of here right
18		now.
19	Whitey:	No—I'm sorry, I'm sorry. I don't know why I
20		shouted. I'm very confused, Vi. You've got to
21		help me. Please don't ask me to leave. Please, Vi.
22		Please.
23	Vi:	Then tell me the truth. I know there's a part of
24		your story that you haven't told me yet. What is
25		it, Whitey?
26	Whitey:	You're right, Vi. I haven't been honest with you.
27		I guess I have to tell you everything—but then
28		I know you'll want me to leave.
29	Vi:	If you tell the whole truth, and you stay calm, I
30		will not tell you to leave.
31	Whitey:	All right. I'll start at the beginning.

Now double-check your answers in Part C and compare your answers with a partner's.

D Improvisation

Work in pairs to prepare the following role-playing activity. Practice your scene, and then you can act it out.

You are two friends. One of you lied to the other about something, and he or she has just discovered the truth. Let's hear your conversation!

E Themes

In small groups or as a whole class, discuss your answers to these questions:

1. Have you (or has someone you know) ever had an experience with the police? If so, tell what happened.
2. Can you remember experiences that happened when you were very young? What is the youngest age that you can remember? What do you remember?

F Spotlight 1

Scanning for Synonyms and Antonyms

PART ONE

Work with a partner. Look in the script for Scene 4 to find words or phrases with these meanings. Also, write the number of the line where you find the word.

1. must _____ (line ____)
2. mixed up _____ (line ____)
3. truthful _____ (line ____)
4. suppose _____ (line ____)
5. relaxed (adjective) _____ (line ____)

6. trust _____ (line ____)
7. couch _____ (line ____)
8. scared _____ (line ____)
9. leave _____ (line ____)
10. yelled _____ (line ____)

PART TWO

*Now look for words or phrases that are the **opposites** of these meanings.*

1. old _____ (line ____)
2. end (verb) _____ (line ____)
3. end (noun) _____ (line ____)
4. ugly _____ (line ____)

5. stand up _____ (line ____)
6. lie (noun) _____ (line ____)
7. that _____ (line ____)
8. right _____ (line ____)

G Overture

Before you listen to the song, look at the picture below. Try to guess what Whitey will sing about. How is he feeling? Why do you think so? Discuss your ideas as a whole class.

H Song

Now listen to the song and fill in the missing **verb forms** and **auxiliaries**. You may listen as many times as you like.

Late Last Night

Whitey:

1   Late last night,
2   All the world _____.
3   Late last night,
4   I _____ my life _____ an illusion.
5   Ev'rything I _____ became confusion,
6   Late last night.

7   Late last night,
8   Under the moon,
9   Late last night,
10 In the darkness I _____ my sense of timing.
11 Someone _____ my name, and bells _____ chiming,
12 Late last night.

13 And the skies _____ _____ gray,
14 And I'll never _____ the same.
15 And I _____ so far away
16 Since the nightmare _____.

17 Late last night,
18 _____ my mind.
19 Late last night,
20 Stars _____ _____, and winds _____ all around me,
21 Spinning me so fast till madness _____ me,
22 Late last night,
23 Late last night.

I Reviews

Discuss your answers to these questions with the whole class.

1. How did Whitey feel late last night? Does his song tell us exactly what happened to him?
2. Tell about a *nightmare* (a bad dream) that you or someone you know has had.
3. Tell about an experience that completely changed your life.

J *Spotlight 2*

The Sounds of *a*

Here are some words from the song that have the letter *a*. The five groups show *five different pronunciations* of *a*. At the top of each list is a word that shows the pronunciation. The underlined part of that word sounds like the bold *a* in the words below it.

d<u>ay</u>	h<u>a</u>t	s<u>aw</u>	<u>u</u>p	c<u>a</u>r	th<u>e</u>re
late changed became name	last laughing fast madness	all called	was away	darkness are far stars	nightmare

PART ONE

*Work with a partner. Try to put the following words with **a** in the correct list below.*

cat / care / make / around / park / ball / baby / share / map / calm / again / fall

d<u>ay</u>	h<u>a</u>t	s<u>aw</u>	<u>u</u>p	c<u>a</u>r	th<u>e</u>re

PART TWO

*Continue to work with a partner. Try to put these words in the correct list below. This exercise is more difficult because the words are written with **a, e, i, o,** and **u.** But the vowel sounds are the same as in Part One.*

wait / hair / love / ran / father / long / late / scared / mother / God / story / add

d<u>ay</u>	h<u>a</u>t	s<u>aw</u>	<u>u</u>p	c<u>ar</u>	th<u>ere</u>

K Finale

Guess *what happened to Whitey late last night. Listen to the song again to get ideas. Write your story here.*

_____
_____
_____
_____
_____
_____
_____
_____
_____
_____
_____
_____
_____
_____
_____
_____

When you finish, share your story with your classmates.

✎ Scene 5 ✎

MIND GAME

A Previews

1. With a partner, **talk** about what you see in the picture on the next page. **Guess** what's happening.
2. By yourself, **write** a paragraph about the picture.

_____
_____
_____
_____
_____
_____
_____
_____
_____
_____

3. When you finish, **exchange** paragraphs with your partner. **Read** your partner's paragraph and **check** for errors. If you don't understand something, **ask** your partner about it. If you find a mistake, help your partner to **fix** it.

B Cues

Your teacher will read some sentences. You will hear these words in the next scene. **Listen carefully** *and circle the letter of the sentence or phrase that you hear. Your teacher will say each one twice.*

1. a. I know how I am.
   b. I know who I am.
   c. I'm now who I am.

2. a. Here's a new car.
   b. He's in a the car.
   c. He was in a car.

3. a. I was walking home.
   b. I wasn't walking home.
   c. Al is walking home.

4. a. That's where the only troubles begin.
   b. That's when all my troubles began.
   c. Dad saw all my troubles began.

5. a. What could I offer you?
   b. Where can I go for you?
   c. What can I do for you?

6. a. I'm a close friend.
   b. I'm close to your friend.
   c. I'm your closest friend.

7. a. I have some import businesses.
   b. I have some port businesses.
   c. I have some important business.

8. a. I would like your company.
   b. I would like you to come with me.
   c. I wasn't lucky you came with me.

9. a. I'm not getting a tiny car.
   b. I'm not going to take a car.
   c. I'm not getting into any car.

10. a. Look over me.
    b. Let go of me.
    c. Like all of me.

Your teacher will tell you the answers and may ask you to **repeat** *sentences that were difficult for you to hear correctly.*

C Scene

Listening for Details

First read the seven questions below. Then listen to the scene two times, and then circle **a**, **b**, **c**, *or* **d**.

1. Where was Whitey planning to go when the man followed him?

   a. To work. b. Home. c. To his car. d. To a hotel.

2. What name did the man call Whitey?

   a. Bill Loos   b. Bill Lewis   c. Paul Ruiz   d. Paul Lewis

3. What is the man's name?

   a. Fred Lachoy   b. Pink Laugh Toy   c. Frank Lovejoy   d. Frank Lachoy

4. Who did the man say he was?

   a. Whitey's father.   b. Whitey's friend.   c. Whitey's father's friend.

5. What did the man say he wanted to discuss?

   a. Business.   b. A car.   c. A hotel.   d. Whitey's father.

6. How far away was the hotel?

   a. A few miles.   b. A few hours.   c. A few blocks.   d. The man didn't say.

7. How did the man want to go to the hotel?

   a. In his limousine.   b. By taxi.   c. By walking.   d. In Whitey's car.

Listening to Make Inferences and Draw Conclusions

Circle True *or* False, *according to the information in this scene. You may listen again if you need to.*

8. At the beginning of the scene, Vi understands Whitey very well.	True	False
9. Whitey is confused by what happened last night.	True	False
10. Whitey feels that he has a problem now.	True	False
11. The man knew Whitey's real name.	True	False
12. Whitey knew this man before last night.	True	False
13. Whitey wanted to hear everything that the man wanted to say.	True	False
14. The man forced Whitey to go with him.	True	False

Now listen for the last time while you follow the script below.

Scene 5

1	Whitey:	I know who I am. Or maybe I should say I know
2		who I was. Right now I really am nobody.
3	Vi:	I don't follow you.
4	Whitey:	Well, late last night somebody else *did* follow me.
5		He was in a car, and I was walking home.
6		That's when all my troubles began . . .

[Street sounds. A car door opens and closes, and someone runs.]

7	Man:	Paul Lewis?
8	Whitey:	Yes, what can I do for you?
9	Man:	My name is Frank Lovejoy. I'm a close friend of
10		your father's. I have some important business to
11		discuss with you, and I would like you to come
12		with me to my hotel. It's just a few blocks from
13		here, but my limousine will take us—
14	Whitey:	Wait a minute. Slow down, slow down. I'm not
15		getting into any car with you. I don't know
16		what you're talking about, and I think you're
17		pretty crazy to think that I'd—Hey! Let go
18		of me! Help! Help!

[The car door closes and they drive away.]

Now double-check your answers in Part C and compare your answers with a partner's.

D Improvisation

Work with a partner to prepare the following role-playing activity. Practice your scene, and then you can act it out for the class.

One of you is Whitey and the other is Frank Lovejoy. Imagine that you are in Frank's limousine, on the way to the hotel. Let's hear your conversation!

E Themes

In small groups or as a whole class, discuss your answers to these questions:

1. Tell about a time when you were very afraid.
2. Whitey is confused about who he is. How about you? Do you know who you are? Of course, you are a student of English. But what else are you? Complete this sentence with your *first* reaction:

Most of all, I am _____.

F Spotlight 1

Scanning for Homonyms

*Work with a partner. Look in the script for Scene 5 to find words that **sound exactly the same** as the words below. Also, write the number of the line where you find the word with the same pronunciation. (Some of the words below will probably be new for you. If you wish, you may check a dictionary for help with the pronunciation and meaning.)*

1. no _____ (line ____)
2. sum _____ (line ____)
3. weight _____ (line ____)
4. your _____ (line ____)
5. wood _____ (line ____)
6. four _____ (line ____)
7. hear _____ (line ____)
8. write _____ (line ____)
9. two _____ (line ____)
10. oar _____ (line ____)
11. inn _____ (line ____)
12. knot _____ (line ____)
13. dew _____ (line ____)
14. ewe _____ (line ____)
15. awl _____ (line ____)

G Overture

Before you listen to the song, look at the picture below. Try to **guess** what Frank Lovejoy will sing to Whitey about. How are they feeling? Why do you think so? Discuss your ideas as a whole class.

Order Card

ISBN	Title	Qty.	Price Each	Total
0-02-307592-9	Beckerman: GUESSWORKS!		$13.00	
	CASSETTE			
	Sales Tax (where applicable)			
	Shipping & Handling			$2.50
	International shipping add			$3.00
			Total	

Payment:

☐ Check for $_____ enclosed and payable to Collier Macmillan.

☐ AMEX ☐ MC ☐ VISA

|_|_|_|_|_|_|_|_|_|_|_|_|_|_|_|_|

(List ALL numbers incl. MC bank number)

Exp. Date _____

Signature _____

(Order not valid without signature)

Mail to: Macmillan Publishing Company
Order Editing Department
Front and Brown Streets
Riverside, New Jersey 08075

Ship to: PLEASE PRINT

First Name _____ Last Name _____

Address _____

City _____ State _____

Country _____ Zip _____

Prices subject to change. Charge orders subject to credit approval.

ESL Dept., 866 Third Ave., New York, N.Y. 10022

| PSR-PSL/300-395 ROY 9 | | FC 001 |

MAILING INSTRUCTIONS

■ Mail this card in an envelope with your check or with your credit card number printed on the front of this card.

■ If you use a credit card, don't forget to include your signature.

Other books with cassettes from Collier Macmillan:

Listening   LET'S LAUGH TOGETHER
by Finger/Barnes
Text ISBN: 0-02-337670-8
Cassettes (2): 0-02-337680-5

GUESSWORKS
by Beckerman
Text ISBN: 0-02-307591-0
Cassette: 0-02-307592-9

THE ENGLISH WORKOUT
by Kelty
Text ISBN: 0-02-362721-2
Cassette: 0-02-362971-1

ON STAGE WITH ENGLISH
by Gilman
Text ISBN: 0-02-343600-X
Cassette: 0-02-343610-7

ON SPEAKING TERMS   2 / e
by Harris/Hube/Vogel
Text ISBN: 0-02-350510-9
Cassette: 0-02-350511-7

Speaking   SAY IT CLEARLY by English
Text ISBN: 0-02-333820-2
Cassette: 0-02-333840-7

Mail to: Macmillan Publishing Company
Order Editing Department
Front and Brown Streets
Riverside, New Jersey 08075

H Song

Now listen to the song and fill in the missing **prepositions** and **articles**. You may listen as many times as you like.

Mind Game

Frank Lovejoy:

1   I know you

2   Better than you know yourself.

3   And if you ride _____ me,

4   You're gonna find your pride _____ me.

5   Come _____ and side _____ me

6   _____ _____ mind game,

7   International mind game.

8   _____ _____ while

9   I will give _____ little clue.

10   And you will understand

11   The life you live has all been planned.

12   Deep _____ _____ distant land,

13   Join _____ mind game,

14   International mind game.

15   You're gonna be _____ shining star

16   _____ _____ winning team.

17   And you will travel very far

18   When you fly _____ _____ dream.

19   Take _____ chance.

20   You can open _____ your eyes,

21   And I can turn _____ key.

22   You're gonna love this mystery.

23   And soon _____ world will see

24   We are just beginning.

25   Place your bet _____ winning

26   _____ mind game,

27   International mind game.

28   Do you, do you, do you,

29   Do you, do you, do you,

30   Mind?

I Reviews

Discuss your answers to these questions with the whole class.

1. What is the "international mind game" that Frank Lovejoy refers to? Try to *guess*.
2. Why does he want to talk to Whitey about it, and how will Whitey respond? *Guess again!*

J Spotlight 2

Gonna

In lines 4, 15, and 22 of the song, Frank sings *gonna*. It means *going to* and is the usual pronunciation of the future auxiliary *(be) going to*. We don't use *gonna* in formal writing, but we do see it often in songs, in advertising, and in scripts. And *gonna* is very frequent—and correct—in conversation.

It is important to know that we never say *gonna* when *going* is a main verb followed by the preposition *to*. Compare these sentences:

1. Whitey is *going to* arrive at the hotel.
2. Whitey is *going to* the hotel.

In sentence 1, we may say *gonna* because *going to* is part of the future auxiliary. The main verb is *arrive*. Sentence 1 means the same as **Whitey will arrive at the hotel**.

But in sentence 2, **going** is the main verb, and so we must pronounce it completely. We may not say **gonna** in sentence 2.

---

*Work with a partner. Practice reading the following paragraphs aloud. Use the **gonna** pronunciation where it is correct.*

Whitey is going with Frank to the hotel. Whitey doesn't know exactly why they are going there, but Frank is probably going to talk to him about the international mind game. And Whitey is going to find out more about the important business that Frank wants to discuss.

The car is going more slowly now. They're going to stop. Frank is going to open the car door. Is Whitey going to try to run away? No. They're going to Frank's room. Whitey's not going to fight. He's going to listen. And then he's going home. Maybe.

K Finale

Work with a partner. Write a scene in Frank Lovejoy's hotel room.

Whitey:

Frank:

Whitey:

Frank:

Whitey:

Frank:

Whitey:

Frank:

Whitey:

Frank:

Whitey:

Frank:

Whitey:

Frank:

When you finish, share your scenes with your other classmates.

I AM NOT THE MAN

A Previews

1. With a partner, **talk** about what you see in the picture on the next page. **Guess** what's happening.
2. By yourself, **write** a paragraph about the picture.

_____

_____

_____

_____

_____

_____

_____

_____

_____

_____

3. When you finish, **exchange** paragraphs with your partner. **Read** your partner's paragraph and **check** for errors. If you don't understand something, **ask** your partner about it. If you find a mistake, help your partner to **fix** it.

B Cues

Your teacher will read some sentences. You will hear these words in the next scene. **Listen carefully** *and circle the letter of the sentence that you hear. Your teacher will say each one twice.*

1. a. Do I take you?
   b. Do we take you?
   c. Did he take you?

2. a. Were you frightened?
   b. Are you frightened?
   c. Where were you frightened?

3. a. Do you scream?
   b. Did you scream?
   c. Did he scream?

4. a. What did he do?
   b. What do you do?
   c. What did you do?

5. a. I can't believe this.
   b. I can believe this.
   c. I can leave this.

6. a. What did I say?
   b. What do you say?
   c. What did he say?

7. a. What did he want?
   b. What do you want?
   c. What did they want?

8. a. What did he mean?
   b. What do you mean?
   c. What did you mean?

9. a. I won't get it.
   b. I don't get it.
   c. I'll go and get it.

10. a. What do you think?
    b. What are you thinking?
    c. What's your thing?

Your teacher will tell you the answers and may ask you to **repeat** *sentences that were difficult for you to hear correctly.*

C Scene

Listening to Make Inferences and Draw Conclusions

First read the seven statements below. Then listen to the scene two times and circle True or False.

1. Vi is very curious to hear Whitey's story.   True   False
2. Whitey doesn't want to tell her anything.   True   False

3. According to Frank, Whitey wasn't a U.S. citizen when he was born. True   False
4. According to Frank, Whitey didn't know his real parents. True   False
5. Frank thought that Whitey might try to leave the hotel room. True   False
6. Vi feels sure that Whitey is not a spy. True   False
7. It is clear that Whitey really is a spy. True   False

Listening for Details

*Listen to the scene again, and then choose the correct answers. Circle **a**, **b**, **c**, or **d** in questions 8, 9, and 11.*

8. What was the name of the hotel?

   a. The Hilton.   b. The Pleasure.   c. The Plaza.   d. The Sheraton.

9. According to Frank, at what age did Whitey arrive in the U.S.?

   a. Two years.   b. Three weeks.   c. Two weeks.   d. Three years.

10. Vi asks Whitey lots of questions. Whitey asks Vi only two. Write Whitey's two questions here.

    a. _____

    b. _____

Listening for Tone

11. At the end of the scene, Vi says, "Uh-oh."
    This expression shows that _____.

    a. something is surprising   c. there might be a problem
    b. time is passing too quickly   d. it's difficult to think

Now listen for the last time while you follow the script below.

Scene 6

1	Vi:	Oh, my God! Did he hurt you?
2	Whitey:	No, but—
3	Vi:	Did he take you to his hotel?
4	Whitey:	Yes, and—
5	Vi:	Why did he call you Paul Lewis?
6	Whitey:	Well, I—
7	Vi:	Were you frightened? Did you scream?
8		What did you do?
9	Whitey:	Do you really want to know?
10	Vi:	Yes!
11	Whitey:	O.K. I'll tell you.
12	Vi:	I can't believe this.
13	Whitey:	Neither can I. We drove to the Plaza Hotel,
14		went up to his room, and he locked us in.
15	Vi:	What did he say? What did he want? Tell me,
16		Whitey. Tell me!
17	Whitey:	He said that I wasn't born in this country.
18	Vi:	What?
19	Whitey:	He said that my parents weren't my parents.
20	Vi:	What do you mean?
21	Whitey:	He told me that my real parents sent me here
22		when I was two weeks old.
23	Vi:	Why?
24	Whitey:	To grow up in an American family.
25	Vi:	I don't get it.
26	Whitey:	They wanted me to be part of their secret
27		international plan!
28	Vi:	Are you . . . a spy?
29	Whitey:	What do you think?
30	Vi:	Uh-oh.

Now double-check your answers in Part C and compare your answers with a partner's.

D Improvisation

1. Work with a group to prepare a list of more questions that you would like to ask Whitey.
2. Now choose one student in the group to be Whitey. Ask him your questions, and listen to his answers!

E Themes

1. Whitey hears that he is not really an American. In your opinion, what things are typically American? Make a list of **objects**, **places**, **people**, and **actions** that you think are **very American**.

   _____ _____ _____ _____

   _____ _____ _____ _____

   When you finish, compare your list with a group's.

2. Make a list of **objects**, **places**, **people**, and **actions** you think are typical **of your native country**.

   _____ _____ _____ _____

   _____ _____ _____ _____

   Share this list with your class.

F Spotlight 1

Get

In line 25 of the scene, Vi says, "I don't get it." In this sentence, **get** means **understand**. The verb **get** has many meanings:

1. I **get** what you're saying, but I don't agree with you.   (get = understand)
2. What will you **get** him for his birthday?   (get = buy)
3. I'm sure that he'll **get** many interesting gifts for his birthday.   (get = receive)
4. What time did you **get** home?   (get = arrive)
5. I hope you don't **get** angry. [**get** + adjective]   (get = become)
6. He will **get** arrested if the police catch him.   (get = be)

   [In sentence 6, we use **get** instead of **be** to show that the subject **has some responsibility**; if we say, "He will **be** arrested," we are not saying anything about his guilt or innocence.

Although these meanings seem very different, they are similar in one way: In each case, the *subject* of the verb **get** changes in some way—physically, mentally, or emotionally.

Work with a partner. Try to write new sentences for each meaning of **get**. Use any tense form.

1. _____   4. _____
2. _____   5. _____
3. _____   6. _____

G Overture

Before you listen to the song, look at the picture below. Try to **guess** *what Whitey will sing about. How is he feeling? Why do you think so? Discuss your ideas as a whole class.*

H Song

Now listen to the song and fill in the missing **verb forms** *and* **auxiliaries**. *You may listen as many times as you like.*

I Am Not the Man

Whitey:

1 Poor me! Poor me!
2 I am not the man that I thought I was.
3 I _____ _____ in the U.S.A.
4 I am not the man that I thought I was,
5 As I _____ earlier today.

6 I _____ not come
7 From the land of instant burgers on buns.
8 I _____ call "home" the nation
9 Of sensational grand-slam home runs.

10 Poor me! Poor me!
11 I am not the man that I thought I was.
12 I _____ _____ in the U.S.A.
13 I am not the man that I thought I was,
14 So I _____ _____ quite suddenly today.

15 I _____ not come
16 From the country of the red, white, and blue.
17 I _____ _____ apple pie
18 Or run to buy a Cadillac — _____ you?

19 Poor me! Poor me!
20 I am not the man that I thought I was.
21 I _____ _____ in the U.S.A.

22	I am not the man that I thought I was.
23	I really _____ _____ who I am today!
24	I _____ _____
25	In the home of country music and jazz.
26	I love the dollar bill,
27	I love the thrill the New York subway _____.
28	Poor me! Poor me!
29	I am not the man that I thought I was.
30	I _____ _____ in the U.S.A.
31	I am not the man that I thought I was.
32	You _____, I'm someone un-American today!

I Reviews

Discuss your answers to these questions with the whole class.

1. According to this song, does Whitey believe what Frank told him in the hotel?
2. What are the differences between Whitey's list of "American things" and the list you made in Part E?
3. In line 27, Whitey indicates that for him, the New York subway is a *thrill*—something very exciting. What is the greatest *thrill* that you have had in the past month? In the past year? In your life?

J Spotlight 2
Scanning for Synonyms

Work with a partner. Look in the song lyrics to find words or phrases with these meanings. Also, write the number of the line where you find the word.

1. found out _____ (line ____)
2. very _____ (line ____)
3. nation _____ (line ____)

4. possesses _____ (line _____)
5. exciting _____ (line _____)
6. immediate _____ (line _____)
7. truly _____ (line _____)
8. unexpectedly _____ (line _____)
9. am unable to _____ (line _____)
10. adore _____ (line _____)
11. unfortunate _____ (line _____)
12. region _____ (line _____)

K Finale

Work with a partner. **Guess** *more about the scene between Whitey and Frank in the hotel room, and write their dialogue here.*

Whitey:

Frank:

Whitey:

Frank:

Whitey:

Frank:

Whitey:

Frank:

Whitey:

Frank:

Whitey:

Frank:

Whitey:

Frank:

When you finish, share your scenes with your other classmates.

MAGIC BOY

A Previews

1. With a partner, **talk** about what you see in the picture on the next page. **Guess** what's happening.
2. By yourself, **write** a paragraph about the picture.

_____
_____
_____
_____
_____
_____
_____
_____
_____
_____

3. When you finish, **exchange** paragraphs with your partner. **Read** your partner's paragraph and **check** for errors. If you don't understand something, **ask** your partner about it. If you find a mistake, help your partner to **fix** it.

B Cues

*Your teacher will read some sentences or phrases. You will hear these words in the next scene. **Listen carefully** and circle the letter of the sentence or phrase that you hear. Your teacher will say each one twice.*

1. a. I don't know what I believe.
   b. I don't know what to believe.
   c. I don't know what you believe.

2. a. I began to remember.
   b. I begin to remember.
   c. I've begun to remember.

3. a. They didn't have the work.
   b. They didn't have to work.
   c. They didn't after work.

4. a. How did he spend the time?
   b. How did they spend their time?
   c. How do you spend the time?

5. a. Were you close to them?
   b. Where were you close to them?
   c. Were you closed to them?

6. a. There was the work.
   b. That is the work.
   c. That was their work.

7. a. What is he talking about?
   b. What was he talking about?
   c. Why was he taking a pot?

8. a. This is too much.
   b. This is to match.
   c. This is to munch.

9. a. Could you do Anita's things?
   b. Could you do any dusting?
   c. Could you do any of those things?

10. a. Summertimes.
    b. Sometimes.
    c. Some dimes.

*Your teacher will tell you the answers and may ask you to **repeat** sentences that were difficult for you to hear correctly.*

C Scene

Listening for Main Ideas

Read the following statements about Whitey and his parents. Listen to the scene once, and then check (✓) all of the statements that are true. You may listen again if you need to.

1. About Whitey

_____ a. Now he is a spy.
_____ b. He has special powers.
_____ c. He knew magicians when he was a child.
_____ d. He was able to talk to angels when he was a child.

2. About Whitey's parents

_____ a. They were always with him.
_____ b. They couldn't find jobs.
_____ c. They had a lot of money.
_____ d. Their main purpose was to help him develop his mind.
_____ e. They had very few friends.
_____ f. It's possible that they were not his real parents.

Listening for Details

Read the four questions below. Then listen to the scene again, and circle a, b, c, or d.

3. Where had Whitey seen the baby picture before?

   a. In a magician's apartment.
   b. In a fortune-teller's apartment.
   c. In his parent's apartment.
   d. In Vi's apartment.

4. What were the parents' names?

   a. Lewis and Karen Roberts
   b. Robin and Gary Lewis
   c. Robert and Karen Lewis
   d. Wilbert and Catherine Lewis

5. At what age could Whitey communicate with angels?

   a. Twelve. b. Ten. c. Two. d. He doesn't say.

6. Whitey mentions some special powers. Which one *doesn't* he mention?

   a. Mind reading.
   b. Fortune-telling.
   c. Out-of-body traveling.
   d. Mental healing.
   e. Talking to spirits.

Now listen for the last time while you follow the script below.

Scene 7

1	Whitey:	Vi, you don't really believe—
2	Vi:	I don't know *what* to believe.
3	Whitey:	I am not a spy.
4	Vi:	So was this man telling the truth?
5	Whitey:	Well, he had a baby picture of me. There's one
6		just like it hanging in my parents' apartment.
7	Vi:	Your parents?
8	Whitey:	Robert and Karen Lewis.
9	Vi:	You remember!
10	Whitey:	Yes. But as Mr. Lovejoy began to speak to me, I
11		began to remember other things.

◆

12	Frank:	Paul. Think . . . think about your childhood.
13		What kind of work did the Lewises do?
14	Whitey:	Well, they—they were wealthy. They . . . didn't
15		have to work.
16	Frank:	Perhaps not in the usual way. But how did they
17		spend their time? Were you close to them?
18	Whitey:	Very close. They were with me—*all* the time.
19	Frank:	Exactly. *That* was their work. To be sure that you
20		grew up according to our plan.
21	Whitey:	What plan?
22	Frank:	Their job was to develop your mind. To unlock
23		the powers of your brain so that you would be
24		ready for us . . . today! You have special powers,
25		don't you? Don't you?
26	Whitey:	I've never told—How do you know about—

◆

27	Vi:	Whitey, what was he talking about?
28	Whitey:	My parents—I mean the parents that I knew—were
29		very unusual people. With very unusual friends.
30		I grew up in the company of . . . magicians.
31	Vi:	This is too much!
32	Whitey:	Everyone I knew had amazing mental powers.
33	Vi:	W-W-W-What kind of powers?
34	Whitey:	Nothing to be afraid of. Mind reading . . .
35		fortune-telling . . . out-of-body traveling . . .
36		talking to spirits . . . things like that.
37	Vi:	And could *you* do any of those things?
38	Whitey:	Sometimes.
39	Vi:	Really!?
40	Whitey:	Yes, they taught me, they showed me, and by the
41		time I was ten, I was even able to communicate
42		. . . with angels!

Now double-check your answers in Part C and compare your answers with a partner's.

D Improvisation

Work with a partner to prepare the following role-playing activity. Practice your scene, and then you can act it out for the class.

Would you like to communicate with a spirit? Now's your chance! With your partner, choose two famous people of the past—people who are not alive anymore. Each of you will play the part of one of those characters. Have a conversation—as those people. Ask each other some interesting questions about your lives.

E Themes

In small groups or as a whole class, discuss your answers to these questions:

1. Did you have a special talent when you were a child? What could you do better than other children?
2. Complete this sentence with *a*, *b*, or *c*:

   When I was young, my parents _____.

   a. controlled my life too much
   b. gave me too much freedom
   c. controlled my life but also gave me the right amount of freedom

   Give some examples to prove your answer.

3. Tell about someone who has a magic power.

F Spotlight 1

Scanning for Synonyms

Work with a partner. Look in the script for Scene 7 to find words or phrases with these meanings. Also, write the number of the line where you find the word.

1. rich _____ (line ____)
2. typical _____ (line ____)
3. sort _____ (line ____)
4. frightened _____ (line ____)
5. talk _____ (line ____)
6. exactly _____ (line ____)
7. instructed _____ (line ____)
8. surprising _____ (line ____)
9. hard to believe
   (informal) _____ (line ____)
10. abilities _____ (line ____)

G Overture

*Before you listen to the song, look at the picture below. Try to **guess** who will sing and what the song will be about. Discuss your ideas as a whole class.*

H Song

*Now listen to the song and fill in the missing **adjectives**. You may listen as many times as you like.*

Magic Boy

Voices:

1 Magic boy,
2 _____ _____
3 Magic boy,
4 Listen to the voices in the breeze.
5 Magic boy,
6 _____ _____
7 Magic boy,
8 Ask, and we will give you what you please.
9 Do you dream of a _____ carousel?
10 Do you wish for a _____ wishing well?
11 Say a _____ word for a magic toy.
12 Tell us, what's your pleasure, magic boy?

13 Magic boy,
14 _____ _____
15 Magic boy,
16 Listen to the laughter in the skies.
17 Magic boy,
18 _____ _____
19 Magic boy,
20 Ev'ry day will bring a _____ surprise.
21 Are you hoping to find a candy land
22 Where you sing and you dance to a circus band?
23 You will sleep on a cloud, then you'll jump for joy.
24 Live your life in magic,
25 Magic boy!

I Reviews

Discuss your answers to these questions with the whole class.

1. What voices do you think are singing this song?
2. What "magical words" do you know?
3. What would be the perfect gift for you?

J Spotlight 2

Rhymes

Look at the words that rhyme in the song: *breeze* (line 4) rhymes with *please* (line 8); *carousel* (line 9) rhymes with *well* (line 10).

PART ONE

Find four other pairs of words that rhyme in the song.

1. _____ and _____
2. _____ and _____
3. _____ and _____
4. _____ and _____

PART TWO

Work with a partner. Try to think of words that rhyme with each of these words from the song. For each word, list as many rhymes as you can.

1. funny: _____
2. wish: _____
3. word: _____
4. day: _____
5. bring: _____
6. find: _____
7. sleep: _____
8. cloud: _____
9. then: _____
10. life: _____

K *Finale*

*The next scene is the final scene of the play. **Guess** what happens, and write your ideas here. You can choose paragraph or dialogue form.*

_____
_____
_____
_____
_____
_____
_____
_____
_____
_____
_____
_____
_____
_____

_____

_____

_____

_____

_____

_____

_____

Share your guesses with your classmates.

BRING THE WORLD TOGETHER

A Previews

1. With a partner, **talk** about what you see in the picture on the next page. **Guess** what's happening.
2. By yourself, **write** a paragraph about the picture.

_____

_____

_____

_____

_____

_____

_____

_____

_____

3. When you finish, **exchange** paragraphs with your partner. **Read** your partner's paragraph and **check** for errors. If you don't understand something, **ask** your partner about it. If you find a mistake, help your partner to **fix** it.

B Cues

Your teacher will read some sentences or phrases. You will hear these words in the next scene. **Listen carefully** *and circle the letter of the sentence or phrase that you hear. Your teacher will say each one twice.*

1. a. What plane was he taking out?
   b. What plan is he talking about?
   c. What plan was he talking about?

2. a. I want it, you know.
   b. I wanted to know.
   c. I want to know.

3. a. The time is coming.
   b. The time has come.
   c. The time's gone.

4. a. I don't know who I am.
   b. I don't know how I am.
   c. I do know who I am.

5. a. We need your hair.
   b. We need you and her.
   c. We need you here.

6. a. I can listen to you.
   b. I can't listen to you.
   c. I couldn't listen to you.

7. a. Any time to think.
   b. I need time to think.
   c. A neat time to think.

8. a. That's why he's sad.
   b. That's what he said.
   c. That's worry, he said.

9. a. I'll go with you.
   b. I'd go with you.
   c. I go with you.

10. a. We'll belong together.
    b. We'd belong together.
    c. We belong together.

Your teacher will tell you the answers and may ask you to **repeat** *sentences that were difficult for you to hear correctly.*

C Scene

Listening to Make Inferences and to Draw Conclusions

First read the six questions. Then listen to the scene as many times as you need to, and circle a, b, c, or d.

1. What kind of organization do Whitey's parents work for?

   a. International spy. b. World peace. c. Child adoption. d. Armed service.

2. Where is Whitey's real father now?

   a. At the Plaza Hotel.   b. In another country.   c. At Grand Central Station.   d. Dead.

3. What does Frank want Whitey to do?

   a. To help the world with his mental power.   c. To look for his real parents.
   b. To leave the United States immediately.   d. To remember an angel.

4. Why did Whitey leave the hotel room?

   a. He didn't believe anything that Frank said.   c. He felt very confused.
   b. He thought that Frank would hurt him.   d. He wanted to speak to Vi.

5. After he left the Plaza Hotel, which happened first?

   a. He met Vi for the first time.   c. He returned to the hotel.
   b. He went to Vi's apartment.   d. He communicated with an angel.

6. At the end of the scene, what does Whitey decide to do about Frank's plan?

   a. To think about it.   c. To forget about it.
   b. To follow it.   d. To ask Vi about it.

Listening for References

Listen to the scene again. When you hear the sentences below, choose the correct meaning of the words in **bold print**, *and circle **a** or **b**. You may listen again if you need to.*

7. **That**'s what I wanted to know.

   a. about the family   b. about Frank's plan

8. **They** followed me out of the Plaza Hotel.

   a. Frank's words   b. the angels

9. I sat **there** for hours and hours.

   a. at the Plaza Hotel   b. at Grand Central Station

10. And **my family** needs me.

    a. Whitey's real parents   b. everyone on earth

Now listen for the last time while you follow the script below.

Scene 8

1	Vi:	Whitey, what did that man want with you? What
2		plan was he talking about?
3	Whitey:	That's what *I* wanted to know . . .

◆

4	Frank:	And now, Paul . . . The time has come for you
5		to serve your family.
6	Whitey:	Family? I don't have any family. I don't know
7		who I am anymore.
8	Frank:	Paul, listen to me. I am a member of the
9		Mindworks Organization. We are an international
10		group of men and women who are working to
11		bring peace to the earth. And we are using mind
12		power to influence the thoughts of humanity.
13		Your real parents believed in our work so strongly
14		that they gave up their son. And now, we need
15		you here in America as our special agent. You
16		can affect the thoughts of so many people! You
17		just have to use your powers of concentration to
18		send out messages of peace. That is the job we
19		have prepared you for. And you will have the
20		help of angels!
21	Whitey:	I can't listen to you anymore. I need time to think.

[He unlocks the door and starts to run.]

22	Frank:	No, wait!
23	Whitey:	(*from out in the hall, as he runs*) I'll be back when
24		I'm ready!
25	Frank:	Paul! Paul! There is one more thing that I didn't
26		tell you! Paul! Paul! I am — I am — your father!

◆

27	Vi:	Your father?
28	Whitey:	That's what he said. And those words echoed in
29		my brain all the way down thirty-two flights of
30		stairs, and they followed me out of the Plaza
31		Hotel onto the street, into the night. And I ran
32		and I ran until I found myself in Grand Central
33		Station. I sat there for hours and hours. And
34		then, a beautiful woman looked into my eyes,
35		and I—and I—
36	Vi:	Oh, Whitey! Do you believe everything the man
37		said?
38	Whitey:	Yes, I do.
39	Vi:	Then you must go back to the hotel right away.
40		And I'll go with you.
41	Whitey:	Yes, Vi! Now I know my real family is—everyone
42		on earth. And my family needs me. Stay with
43		me, Vi. You can help me.
44	Vi:	Of course I'll stay with you . . . Paul. We belong
45		together!

Now double-check your answers in Part C and compare your answers with a partner's.

D Improvisation

Work with a partner to prepare the following role-playing activity. Practice your scene, and then you can act it out for the class.

One of you is a parent and the other is the child. The parent tells the child some shocking news, and the child reacts.

E Themes

In small groups or as a whole class, discuss the following real-life situations.

1. Tell about a time when you felt like running away.
2. Tell about a big surprise that you have had in your life.

F Spotlight 1

Consonant Sounds/Pronunciation of Regular Past Tense Verbs

The consonant sounds of English can be divided into two groups: *voiceless* (without voice) and *voiced* (with voice). The chart below shows how these sounds fit into the two groups. The pairs of sounds connected with a line (*p* and *b*, *t* and *d*, etc.) are pronounced in the same manner—except that for the voiceless sounds at the left, there is no vibration of the vocal cords. In other words, *p* and *b* are really the same sound—except that for *p*, we do not use our voice; for *b*, we need our voice.

Consonant Sounds

Voiceless	Voiced
p	b
t	d
k	g
f	v
s	z
sh	usually
ch	j
think	this
(x = ks) box	exactly (x = gz)
h	m, n, ng, l, r, w, y
q (= k)	

It is useful to know about voiceless and voiced consonants in order to understand the pronunciation of regular past verbs.

There are three possible pronunciations for the *ed* in the past form of regular verbs:

Group 1 *T*	Group 2 *D*	Group 3 *ED*
helped	opened	needed
kissed	called	waited
picked	loved	started
wished	cared	ended

In Group 1, we pronounce the *ed* as *t*; the correct pronunciation of the first verb is "helpt." In Group 2, we pronounce only the *d*; the pronunciation for the first verb in this group is "opend." Group 3 is the only group in which we pronounce *ed*—although the *e* sounds more like the *i* in *s<u>i</u>t* because it is not in a stressed (strong) syllable.

PART ONE

Work with a group. Together, try to complete the rules about the three different pronunciations of ed. *(Here's some help: You will need to think about voiceless and voiced sounds.)*

Rule 1: We use the *t* pronunciation of *ed* if _____.

Rule 2: We use the *d* pronunciation of *ed* if _____.

Rule 3: We use the *ed* pronunciation of *ed* if _____.

PART TWO

Work with a partner. Look in the script for Scene 8 to find six verbs that end in ed. *Then write them in the correct group below. (Keep in mind that all* **vowel** *sounds are voiced.)*

Group 1 T	Group 2 D	Group 3 ED

PART THREE

1. *Work with a group to prepare an* **ed** *pronunciation quiz for your classmates. On a piece of paper prepare a list of twenty regular past verbs. Be sure to include verbs for all three groups.*
2. *Exchange papers with a different group. Work together to choose the correct pronunciation, and write* **T**, **D**, *or* **ED** *next to each verb.*
3. *When you finish, return the paper to the group that wrote it, and grade each other's papers.*

G Overture

Before you listen to the song, look at the picture below. Try to **guess** what Paul and Vi will sing about. How are they feeling? Why do you think so? Discuss your ideas as a whole class.

H Song

*Now listen to the song, and fill in the missing **phrases**. You may listen as many times as you like.*

Bring the World Together

Paul:

1   I feel my worries all are past.
2   With you, _____ _____ _____ at last.

3   Bring the world together in a smile,
4   _____ _____ _____.
5   Bring the world together _____ _____ _____.
6   It doesn't take a miracle
7   To _____ _____ _____ _____.
8   And it only takes a moment to reveal a wonderland,
9   A family.
10 _____ _____ _____ we belong together.
11 We are a harmony.
12 Bring the world together,
13 Bring the world together.

Vi:

14 I feel my troubles disappear.
15 A rainbow shines _____ _____ _____.

16 Bring the world together in a smile,
17 _____ _____.
18 Bring the world together _____ _____ _____.
19 It doesn't take a miracle to
20 _____ _____ _____ _____.

| 21 | And it only takes a moment to reveal a wonderland, |
| 22 | A family. |

Together:

23	_____ _____ _____ we belong together.
24	We are a harmony.
25	Bring the world together,
26	Bring the world together,
27	Bring the world together.

I Reviews

Discuss your answers to these questions with the whole class.

1. What are some examples of *miracles*?
2. How can we help to "bring the world together." Make some practical suggestions.

J Spotlight 2

Memorizing

Learn to sing the song. Listen to it again as many times as you like. Work with a partner to memorize the words. Then sing it with the whole class—without looking at the lyrics. For homework, teach it to someone you love.

K Finale

Guess what will happen to Paul and Vi, and write your ideas here. You can choose paragraph, dialogue, or song form. And you can choose a happy ending or a sad one. The choice is yours.

_____
_____
_____
_____
_____
_____
_____
_____
_____
_____
_____
_____
_____
_____
_____
_____
_____
_____

The End . . . or Just the Beginning

SHEET MUSIC

Strangers

Words and Music by
HOWARD BECKERMAN

Woman: Stran - gers, are we real - ly hold - ing hands?

Man: Stran - gers, born to be with, good to be Together: stran-gers.

Just Around the Corner

Words and Music by
HOWARD BECKERMAN

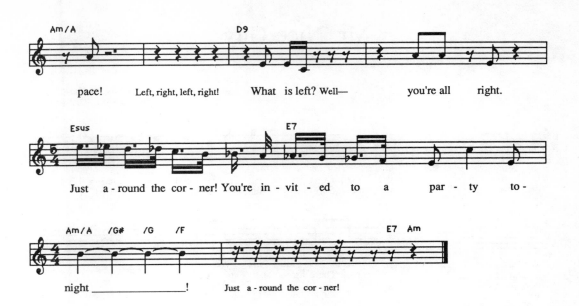

pace!   Left, right, left, right!   What is left? Well—   you're all   right.

Just a - round the cor - ner! You're in - vit - ed to a par - ty to -

night _____!   Just a - round the cor - ner!

Mr. Nice Guy

Words and Music by
HOWARD BECKERMAN

talk   to   me!   If   you   want   a   lit - tle   in - spi - ra - tion,   you'll   a - gree   there   is
talk   to   me! Vi: If   I   want   a   lit - tle   in - spi - ra - tion,   I   can   see   there   is

on — ly   one   com - pan - ion,   and   he's   yours   for   free!   Don't   pass   me   by
on — ly   one   com - pan - ion,   and   he's   mine   for   free! Whitey: Don't   pass   me   by

_____ !   Let   me   be   your   Mis - ter
_____ ! Vi: Let   him   be   your   Mis - ter

1.
Ni   —   i - i - ice   Guy _____ !

2.
Whitey: Let   me   be   your   Mis - ter   Together: Ni   —   i - i

- ice _____   Guy _____ !

Late Last Night

Words and Music by
HOWARD BECKERMAN

night - mare came _____. late last night _____, late last

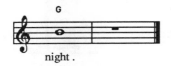

night .

Mind Game

Words and Music by
HOWARD BECKERMAN

I Am Not the Man

Words and Music by
HOWARD BECKERMAN

Whitey: Poor me! Poor me! I am not the man that I
(Poor) me! Poor me! I am not the man that I
(Poor) me! Poor me! I am not the man that I
(Poor) me! Poor me! I am not the man that I

thought I was. I was-n't born in the U. S. A. I am
thought I was. I was-n't born in the U. S. A. I am
thought I was. I was-n't born in the U. S. A. I am
thought I was. I was-n't born in the U. S. A. I am

not the man that I thought I was, as I dis-cov-ered ear-li-er to-
not the man that I thought I was, so I was told quite sud-den-ly to-
not the man that I thought I was. I real-ly don't know who I am to-
not the man that I

day. I do not come from the land of in-stant
day. I do not come from the coun-try of the
day! I don't be-long in the home of coun-try

burg-ers on buns. I can't call "home" the na-tion of sen-sa-tion-
red, white, and blue. I can't eat ap-ple pie or run to buy a
mu-sic and jazz. I love the dol-lar bill, I love the thrill the

al   grand - slam   home   runs.   Poor
Ca - dil - lac— would   you?   Poor
New   York   sub - way   has.   Poor

thought   I   was,   You   see,   I'm

some - one   un   -   Am - er - i - can   to - day !

Magic Boy

Words and Music by
HOWARD BECKERMAN

dream   of a gold - en   car - ou - sel?   Do you wish   for a per - son - al
hop - ing to find   a   can - dy   land where you sing   and you dance   to a

wish - ing   well?   Say   a   mag - i - cal   word _____   for a   mag - ic
cir - cus   band?   You   will   sleep   on   a   cloud _____, then you'll   jump for

toy _____ . Tell   us,   what's   your
joy _____ . Live   your   life   in

pleas - ure,   mag   -   ic
mag - ic,   mag   -

1.

boy _____ ? - ic

2.

boy _____ !

Bring the World Together

Words and Music by
HOWARD BECKERMAN

bring   the world   to - ge - eth - er,

bring   the world   to - ge - eth - er.

ANSWER KEY

Scene 1

B Cues

2) c   3) b   4) a   5) b   6) a   7) c   8) a   9) b   10) b

C Scene

1) c   2) a   3) a, b, d, f, g, j   4) Can you stay with me?

F Spotlight 1

1) alone / line 19   2) nowhere / line 8   3) maybe / line 18   4) strange / line 4   5) excuse / line 1
6) sure / line 6   7) can / line 3   8) O.K. / line 1

H Song

3) feel   4) seeing / see   7) Holding   9) knows / need / stay   11) sing   12) remember   14) know
15) hear   16) play   19) Born   21) shining   25) Discovering   28) sing   29) remember   31) know
32) hear   33) play   36) holding   38) Born

Scene 2

B Cues

1) c   2) b   3) a   4) b   5) c   6) b   7) a   8) c   9) a   10) b

C Scene

1) d 2) d 3) b and c 4) b 5) a 6) b 7) a 8) b 9) b

H Song

1) a 2) an 4) the 5) The 8) an 9) a / for 11) the 12) the 15) in 16) to 17) the
18) to 19) to 22) a 23) a 25) the 33) to a

J Spotlight 2

Part One: 1) d 2) e 3) g 4) f 5) h 6) a 7) c 8) i 9) b

Part Two: 1) I 2) L 3) L 4) I 5) L 6) L 7) L 8) L 9) I

Scene 3

B Cues

1) b 2) c 3) a 4) b 5) b 6) a 7) c 8) a 9) b 10) a

C Scene

1) b 2) d 3) a. Vi asks about Whitey's house. b. Vi suggests going to the police. c. Whitey shouts at Vi. d. Whitey says he will go to the police. e. Whitey asks Vi one question. 4) b
5) b 6) Can I stay at your house tonight? / a

F Spotlight 1

Part One: 1) doesn't remember 2) shouts / won't be 3) 'll find out / go 4) asks / won't want
5) 'll all be / discover 6) leaves / 'll never see 7) will be glad / go 8) are / will remember

H *Song*

1) my   2) you / I'm   4) you   5) me   6) I'm   7) I'm   8) I'm   9) me / you're   10) you   11) me
12) you   13) You'll   15) he's yours   16) me   17) me / your   19) him   20) I / him   21) There's
22) I / him   23) I'm   24) He's   25) I'm   27) him / I'm   28) you   29) me   30) I / I   31) he's
32) me   33) him / your   34) me / your

J *Spotlight 2*

1) companion / line 14 or line 31   2) fun / line 7 or line 24   3) pleasant / line 10 or line 28
4) sincere / line 2   5) incredibly / line 3   6) inspiration / line 12 or line 30   7) safe and sound /
line 9 or line 27   8) around / line 7 or line 24   9) trust / line 19

Scene 4

B *Cues*

1) a   2) c   3) b   4) b   5) a   6) a   7) c   8) b   9) a   10) a

C *Scene*

1) a. cheerful and friendly   b. nervous and surprised   c. afraid   d. angry   e. calm and serious
2) mother / coffee / voice / face   3) a, b, e, and g   4) Why don't you   5) Should I   6) Let's
7) You've got to   8) Please

F *Spotlight 1*

Part One: 1) 've got to / line 20   or   have to / line 27   2) confused / line 20   3) honest / line 26
4) guess / line 27   5) calm / line 29   6) believe / line 13   7) sofa / line 3   8) afraid /
line 17   9) get out / line 17   10) shouted / line 20

Part Two: 1) young / line 5   2) start / line 31   3) beginning / line 31   4) beautiful / line 2
5) sit down / line 3   6) truth / line 23 or line 29   7) this / line 1 or line 14
8) wrong / line 14

H Song

2) changed 4) discovered / was 5) knew 10) lost 11) called / were 13) are looking 14) be
15) feel 16) came 18) Losing 20) were laughing / blew 21) found

J Spotlight 2

Part One:

d<u>ay</u>	h<u>a</u>t	s<u>aw</u>	<u>u</u>p	c<u>ar</u>	th<u>e</u>re
make baby	cat map	ball fall	around again	park calm	care share

Part Two:

d<u>ay</u>	h<u>a</u>t	s<u>aw</u>	<u>u</u>p	c<u>ar</u>	th<u>e</u>re
wait late	ran add	long story	love mother	father God	hair scared

Scene 5

B Cues

1) b 2) c 3) a 4) b 5) c 6) a 7) c 8) b 9) c 10) b

C Scene

1) b 2) d 3) c 4) c 5) a 6) c 7) a 8) False 9) True 10) True 11) True 12) False
13) False 14) True

F Spotlight 1

1) know / line 1 or line 15   2) some / line 10   3) wait / line 14   4) you're / line 16   5) would / line 11   6) for / line 8   7) here / line 13   8) right / line 2   9) to / line 10, line 11, or line 17   10) or / line 1   11) in / line 5   12) not / line 14   13) do / line 8   14) you / line 3, line 8, line 11, or line 15   15) all / line 6

H Song

3) with   4) with   5) on / with   6) In the   8) In a   9) a   12) in a   13) the   15) the   16) On the   18) into the   19) a   20) up   21) the   23) the   25) on   26) The

Scene 6

B Cues

1) c   2) a   3) b   4) c   5) a   6) c   7) a   8) b   9) b   10) a

C Scene

1) True   2) False   3) True   4) True   5) True   6) False   7) False   8) c   9) c   10) a. Do you really want to know?   b. What do you think?   11) c

H Song

3) wasn't born   5) discovered   6) do   8) can't   12) wasn't born   14) was told   15) do   17) can't eat   18) would   21) wasn't born   23) don't know   24) don't belong   27) has   30) wasn't born   32) see

J Spotlight 2

1) discovered / line 5   2) quite / line 14   3) country / line 16   4) has / line 27   5) sensational / line 9   6) instant / line 7   7) really / line 23   8) suddenly / line 14   9) can't / line 8 or line 17   10) love / line 27   11) poor / line 1, line 10, line 19, or line 28   12) land / line 7

Scene 7

B Cues

1) b   2) a   3) b   4) b   5) a   6) c   7) b   8) a   9) c   10) b

C Scene

1) b, c, and d   2) a, c, d, and f   3) c   4) c   5) b   6) d

F Spotlight 1

1) wealthy / line 14   2) usual / line 16   3) kind / line 13   4) afraid / line 34   5) speak / line 10
6) just / line 6   7) taught / line 40   8) amazing / line 32   9) too much / line 31   10) powers /
line 23, line 24, line 32, or line 33

H Song

2) Funny little   6) Quiet little   9) golden   10) personal   11) magical   14) Happy little
18) Silly little   20) new

J Spotlight 2

Part One: 1) toy / boy   2) skies / surprise   3) land / band   4) joy / boy

Part Two: [Here are some possibilities. You may find others.]   1) bunny, money, sunny   2) dish,
fish   3) bird, heard, third   4) may, play, stay   5) king, ring, thing   6) blind, kind,
mind   7) keep, leap, weep   8) crowd, proud   9) again, pen, when   10) knife, wife

Scene 8

B Cues

1) c   2) b   3) b   4) a   5) c   6) b   7) b   8) b   9) a   10) c

C Scene

1) b   2) a   3) a   4) c   5) a   6) b   7) b   8) a   9) b   10) b

F Spotlight 1

Part One: Rule 1) We use the **t** pronunciation of **ed** if the sound before it is voiceless.
Rule 2) We use the **d** pronunciation of **ed** if the sound before it is voiced.
Rule 3) We use the **ed** pronunciation of **ed** if the sound before it is **t** or **d**.

Part Two:

Group 1 T	Group 2 D	Group 3 ED
looked	believed prepared echoed followed	wanted

H Song

2) I'm coming home   4) In a song   5) in a dream   7) take a stranger's hand   10) I know that 15) because you're here   17) In a song   18) in a dream   20) Take a stranger's hand   23) I know that